BEDSIDE MANNERS

*How to support your family and friends
through life's most difficult challenges.*

A SIMPLE GUIDE TO EMPOWERMENT

Monica R. Jarrett

Editor: Helen Kimmelfield
Cover and Interior Design: Anita Jones, Another Jones Graphics
Book production: Joan Pinkert, Another Jones Graphics

Library of Congress Control Number: 2010939680

ISBN: 978-0-615-42005-9

First Edition

Monarch Publications, LLC
PO Box 1548
Fairview, OR 97024

Acknowledgments

My vision is for this book to help support others emotionally, physically and spiritually in their times of need. As I collected the stories and information contained in this book, I came to realize that sharing their stories, and knowing that they might help others, was helping the tellers themselves to heal.

My most heartfelt "Thank you" goes out to all of those who contributed to the creation of this wonderful book. It has been a privilege and an honor to hear your stories and to provide support to others in their times of need.

Thank you to my sister Teresa, for blessing me and others with her knowledge and her special gifts of healing.

Thank you to my supportive and patient husband David, and to my four beautiful children: Madeline, who helped with the graphic designs; Nick, who helped with the technical support; Ben, for his patience in listening to each story after I wrote it, and Michael, the youngest, for his encouragement year after year.

A special "Thank-you" to William and Margaret Ollenbrook, my parents, for teaching me at an early young age that what really matters in life is; faith, family and friends.

BEDSIDE MANNERS
BETWEEN
FAMILY & FRIENDS

One of the most important ways to demonstrate that we care for our loved ones is to provide positive support during negative experiences. Every time we do so, we are given a priceless opportunity to become more compassionate, more empathetic, more loving, more faithful, and more grateful.

Communication styles vary from person to person and can be challenging at times. However, there may be moments when everything clears away and you experience a special kind of communication, a spiritual connection, when no words are spoken and only eyes and touch are communicating. It is a beautiful experience, and amazing to witness.

Remember that every family has its own dynamic, which may or may not be of our choosing. Friends are the family we choose, and as a friend you may see what has been overlooked, and be in a position to assist.

It is an honor to be called to stand by someone in a crisis. It can also be a daunting, even overwhelming experience. This book will give you the tools you need to translate what you feel in your heart into positive action.

CONTENTS

USEFUL TOOLS 🌿

THE BEGINNING

AFTER THE NEWS

Just like the butterfly,
you also hold these qualities:

Transformation

Beauty

Lightness

Endurance

Hope

AFTER THE NEWS

People react in different ways to the upsetting impact of bad news. They may become literally speechless, unable to think clearly, and feel powerless to help. They may leap into action because they cannot bear to sit idle, whether or not it is the best way to help. When you first learn of a loved one's distress, you will need to manage your own emotional upset in an order to be an effective helper.

- Sit down, think for a minute, meditate, and pray on it
- Remain in control; focus on deep and steady breathing
- If you received the news directly, you might ask "Is there anyone I can call for you? Is someone with you?"
- Or, "Would you like me to come over to listen or pick you up and go out and talk?"
- Or, "Would you like me to call a support group, church, or organize a prayer chain?"
- Or simply say, "How can I help you or your family?"

HEAD HELPER (ADVOCATE)

In many cases, it is useful, even necessary, to have one person be the designated head helper, who co-ordinates offers of assistance and delegates tasks. This person is responsible for getting the help required, even to the point of advocating for the individual and/or the family on matters of medical and daily care.

- Find out if someone in particular wishes to take on this responsibility
- If you are the designated head helper, begin by collecting phone numbers of family and friends. Get permission to use personal phone book(s)

- During medical consultations, four ears are better than two. Bring someone along to attend appointments, to take notes and assist with decision-making
- To keep track of treatment plans file copies of medical reports for reference
- List medications if needed
- You may need to ensure that finances are in order: get up-to-date information on utilities, house, loans, etc., including relevant telephone numbers and addresses
- Set up an email system for progress reports, and turn on the answering machine
- Use all the offers of help around you! Delegate! Delegate! Delegate!
- Take 10 minutes or more daily to clear your mind and recharge with positive energy
- Eat right: get enough protein, vegetables, fruit, water, and take multi-vitamins if necessary
- Take naps!
- Listen to music that moves your spirit

- TOOLS: **Medical Information Cards.** Sample at the end of this chapter. (See USEFUL TOOLS section, page 99)

CONFIDENTIALITY

Your friend or relative is hurting and vulnerable, and may entrust you with very private information. You have an obligation to protect other people's privacy, in order to support their emotional and mental well-being.

- Always ask what information may be made public, and what should remain private, and respect the boundaries you are given
- Avoid and discourage gossip, no matter what you want to say, share, or express

- Adopt a positive attitude: avoid dwelling on negative outcomes, and focus on the spiritual growth that difficult experiences can produce

- Absolutely avoid whispering, and negative discussion in the sickroom. Even when they cannot speak, patients can usually hear very well and at least well enough to sense anxiety and pessimism

- If the news or information you receive is too overwhelming for you to keep to yourself, it is time to confide in a professional. Contact a counselor or your pastor

- Whenever children are involved, keep your interaction positive and simple. If you have questions or information, talk to the Head Helper, or Advocate. The children of those in crisis should get medical and personal information from family or medical staff only

COMPASSION

Ask yourself what would be most comforting at that moment to the person you are trying to help, and offer that. Understand that everyone reacts differently to life-altering situations, and that your job is not to fix the problem, but to give appropriate and welcome comfort to the sufferer.

- Hold hands, hug, give back or shoulder-rub

- Pray and /or meditate together; light a candle

- Say, "We will help you"; "I am here for you"; Allow people to share or express their feelings. Understand that the range of reactions is broad: showing fear, anger, discouragement, anxiety, shock, confusion, trembling, weeping and walking back and forth — these are all natural responses. Listen and be present without judgment

- TOOLS — see **Do I Give Emotional or Informational Support**, later in this chapter.

Communication

Perhaps the most important part of the Advocate's job is to monitor and facilitate communication; information should be presented accurately and positively and it should be easy for family and friends to stay in touch. The following suggestions are helpful whether or not you are the Head Helper.

- Set up an E-mail, Website, and/or Blog.
- Be clear on any treatment plan. Ask questions, make notes and double-check as necessary.
- Respond to questions about the future with the good possibilities.
- Maintain a positive attitude, and encourage laughter.
- Tell children and other family members that doctors and medical staff are taking good care their loved one.
- Children need to know that someone will always be there for them, and to be reassured that they are not responsible for what has happened.
- Be sensitive to the fact that talking about your own problems may be overwhelming to your friend or relative at this time.
- Do not downplay or dismiss the seriousness of the situation. Simply sitting and listening without interruption can be incredibly supportive.
- Explain that people want to help, and that all the everyday stuff will be taken care of.
- Assist in sending "Thank you" notes to all those who help out.

What Do I Say?
What Should I Write?

It is more important to acknowledge a painful reality with honest sympathy than to insist that everything is going to be all right or the same as before.

- "We heard about your condition and our thoughts and prayers are with you and your family."
- "I am thinking about you today and every day. Focusing on your speedy recovery."
- "I just heard about your situation and I am here to help in any way I can. My number is (your number here) 24 hours a day."
- "Our family is praying for you every night."
- "How are you? (Listen, listen, and listen!) If you don't mind, I will call once a week to see if you need help."
- "Our thoughts and prayers are with you and your child."
- "May God's grace shine on you and your family."
- "We are wishing you a speedy recovery."
- "I am thinking of you today and everyday at 1:05pm."
- "We just heard about your condition and wish you and yours well."

Do I Give Emotional or
Informational Support?

This section is designed to help you determine what your loved one needs to cope and have a sense of reassurance. In general, people communicate in an emotional or an informational fashion, and they tend to respond best to support offered in the same style, as shown below. Some people may need both types of support, whatever their communication style may be.

Emotional Communication

"I am afraid"

"I feel vulnerable"

"Will others be O.K. in my absence?"

"Will I be the same after this is completed?"

"Is my dog doing well without me?"

"I feel overwhelmed and tired"

Recommendations for those that need **Emotional support**:

- Hold their hand.
- Tuck their blanket in around them adjust their colorful pillow for them.
- Let them know that their concerns are being addressed: "Your pets are being taken care of and the kids have a schedule in place."
- Acknowledge that their feelings are normal for someone in their situation.
- Tell them that people are praying for them and their families.

Informational Communication

"I just need the facts"

"How long will it take for me to be well?"

"Where will I be during recovery"

"Someone needs to tell me what happened during surgery"

"I feel pain, is this normal?"

"Has anyone else experienced this type of problem?"

Recommendations for those who need **Informational support**:

- It's O.K. to ask doctor, nurses, and other medical staff questions about: treatment plans, recovery, visitation, pain management, and recovery time.
- Write down everything. Use a note pad and make out a question list; write down the answers, and keep track of who told you what.
- Make sure your loved ones have the information they need.
- Educate yourself and your loved one on the topic and or treatment.

Pain Scale

This scale can be used by your loved one to communicate his or her degree of pain or discomfort.

No Pain	Least Pain	Mild Pain	Moderate	Severe	Unbearable

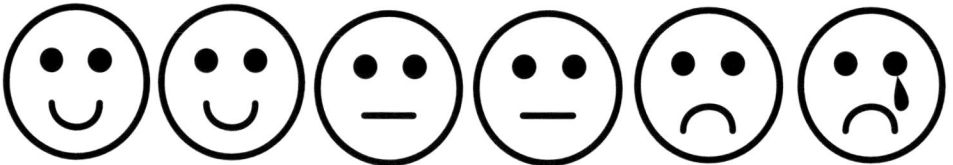

| 0 | 1 | 2 | 3 | 4 | 5 | 6 | 7 | 8 | 9 | 10 |

A SUMMARY OF BASIC BEDSIDE MANNERS

The following suggestions provide welcome support, whatever the specific situation may be.

- Acknowledge the reality of the situation
- Keep in touch: visit, call, send cards, using positive language
- Send flowers, plants, fruit basket, inspirational cards
- Pray and meditate for loved ones
- Educate yourself and others about the specifics of the situation — get the facts
- Help with meals: prepare them; buy gift cards and/or groceries (See **Meal Calendar** in USEFUL TOOLS, page 92)
- Help with the day-to-day family business: pick up and deliver children to school or caregivers; take care of pets (See **Care Calendar** in USEFUL TOOLS, page 89)
- Help with yard work: mow lawn; plant flowers; pull weeds. (See **Care Calendar**, USEFUL TOOLS, page 89)
- Provide additional transportation: to appointments, to stores, to church. (See **Care Calendar**, USEFUL TOOLS, page 89)
- Be a good listener. Don't interrupt, and don't argue — your job is to provide a sympathetic ear, not to be a distraction
- Help with bills: either directly, with payments, or organize fundraisers. (See **Fundraising Ideas,** USEFUL TOOLS, page 90)
- Be patient and kind
- Avoid telling tragic stories with bad endings!
- Avoid talking about your problems, and bringing additional stress to loved one
- Avoid using clichés: "Be tough"; "It's no big deal"; "The worst is yet to come"
- Avoid gossip!
- Don't miss an opportunity to say "I love you"
- Be in the moment!
- Write a letter to God and mail it
- Expect a miracle!

IMPORTANT MEDICAL INFORMATION

Below are reduced versions of the medical information cards that should be organized and kept available. Full size versions of these are in the USEFUL TOOLS section on page 99.

PRIMARY CARE PHYSICIAN
Name _____
Hospital/Clinic _____
Phone _____
Fax _____
Address _____
Email _____

PHARMACY
Pharmacy _____
Phone _____
Fax _____
Address _____
Email _____
Account Number _____

SPECIALIST
Name/Specialty _____
Hospital/Clinic _____
Phone _____
Fax _____
Address _____
Email _____

SPECIALIST
Name/Specialty _____
Hospital/Clinic _____
Phone _____
Fax _____
Address _____
Email _____

HEALTH INSURANCE
Company Name _____
Agent's Name _____
Phone _____
Fax _____
Address _____
ID# _____

SECONDARY HEALTH INSURNACE
Company Name _____
Agent's Name _____
Phone _____
Fax _____
Address _____
ID# _____

ADVANCE DIRECTIVE/ORGAN DONOR
Person who has the Advance Directive _____
_____
Phone _____
Oregon Donor Information _____
_____

EMERGENCY CONTACTS
Name _____
Phone _____
Name _____
Phone _____
Name _____
Phone _____

LIFE CHALLENGES

ADDICTIONS

Recovery from addiction requires hard work, a proper attitude and learning skills to stay sober, not drinking alcohol or using other drugs. Successful drug recovery or alcohol recovery involves changing attitudes, acquiring knowledge, and developing skills to meet the many challenges of sobriety.

—DENNIS DALEY, PHD

ALCOHOLISM

Our soldier came home from his term in Afghanistan. He was on high alert, unable to find a sense of peace. I quickly learned that he had become addicted to alcohol to deal with the unstable emotions that he was experiencing. One particular day, I approached two police officers and asked them how I could get help for my son. I told them about the situation and my feeling of helplessness. Come to learn they too are veterans. They had information about a support group, and suggested I go to the local recruiting office and request fellow service people to attend an intervention session. So I did. As my son and our family walk into the intervention office, we see that there are three service people and one of the police officers there to support our son in his recovery. It was such a powerful moment in our lives and it worked. Our son received help and is now alcohol-free, thanks to the support of his fellow soldiers and everyone else around him.

—FATHER OF A UNITED STATES SOLDIER

METHAMPHETAMINES

After many years of using meth, I longed to be free of drugs. I had been to many meetings and had gone through a diversion program. During that time, I guess, I wasn't ready to quit. My spirit was crying out for more help. I called my faithful grandmother and told her that my daughter and I needed to stay with her. She welcomed me into her home. She prepared healthy meals to support my body as I healed from my addictions. Over time my grandmother and I knew that I was on the road to recovery and would be freed of my addictions.

—JILL

~ ✾ ~

BEDSIDE MANNERS:

- Encourage medical attention, drive loved one to clinic or hospital
- Educate yourself: use the internet to get information about addiction (see websites below)
- Self-inflicted harm by your loved one may be a serious cry for help. Seek medical attention immediately
- Encourage counseling to improve the mental health of individual and/or the whole family
- If the addicted person refuses to get help, you should acquire useful tools to help your loved one by attending counseling yourself
- Assist in recovery, not in enabling, your loved one
- Provide a safe place for your loved one, away from others with addictions
- Make sure any children involved are in a safe environment
- Provide healthy meals for consistent physical support
- Team up for a physical exercise program (Check with doctor)
- Schedule conference calls or video chat with family and/or friends to stay connected with loved one and each other
- Consider creating a routine to pray together
- Use **Monthly Support Calendar** (See USEFUL TOOLS, page 98)

- Help with basic household chores; paint a picture together; plant a garden together; tell your loved one that you are there and that you care
- Help with positive changes, keep supportive routines in place
- All medications in the home should be stored in a locked cabinet
- Instead of giving money to directly to your loved one, pay bills for food, shelter, and counseling
- Remember, when a person is on drugs, you are talking to the drugs, not the person
- Stay focused on positive mission and outcome
- Avoid negative statements like these:
  - You're hopeless
  - I have given up on you
  - Where is your head?
  - You are a loser
  - Are you stupid?
  - You're just fat

Resources:

- Narcotic Anonymous: *www.na.org*
- Alcoholics Anonymous: *www.aa.org*
- Centers for Disease and Prevention Control: *www.cdc.gov/obesity/*
- National Council on Problem Gambling: *www.ncpgambling.org*
- Mayo Clinic: *www.mayoclinic.com*

Cancer

If children have the ability to ignore all odds and percentages,

then maybe we can all learn from them. When you think about it,

what other choice is there but to hope?

We have two options, medically and emotionally:

give up, or fight like hell.

— Lance Armstrong

BREAST CANCER

A diagnosis of cancer and its treatment can be "stripping". I lost my security, my hair, my mind, my health, my strength, my ability to sleep and to regulate temperature, and my sense of smell and taste. Touch was really the only thing unaffected. My family found the softest, most comforting robe and clothes for me as treatment progressed. That tactile softness was warm and comforting.

— KRISTIN O. _

LEUKEMIA

When I was diagnosed with cancer I felt numb for a few minutes; so many thoughts were going through my mind. The strongest thought that I experienced was: cancer will be no threat to me. I will be with people that will provide positive support and hold

the same vision of my healthy future. I will be on a journey and my unwavering faith will carry me through. It has worked thus far!

DEDICATED TO ED TRIBBY

LUNG CANCER

On a day that my Aunt was feeling well, I ask her if she would like to take a stroll in her wheelchair around the neighborhood. To my surprise she said, "I would love to". She enjoyed it very much; we laughed, we stopped and watched people working in their yards, and we could smell the fresh cut grass, the cedar chips around the flower beds and hear the sound of sprinklers watering the gardens. The blue sky felt like a cool blanket around us and the sun warmed our faces. We took the time to notice that the little things around us make a big difference. This simple afternoon has and will be cherished in my heart and mind forever.

DEDICATED TO THE MOLLAHANS'

~ ❦ ~

BEDSIDE MANNERS:

- Send cards filled with positive words, inspirational poems, prayers of healing
- Send flowers, fruit basket or plants only if allowed (oncology staff may decline for patient's welfare)
- Offer to drive and sit with loved one at appointments and or treatments
- Offer to be the second set of ears at doctor appointments and bring a note pad with your questions about details of treatment plans
- Use medication pill box to help organize different medications
- Educate yourself and loved one about the latest research, studies, papers, testimonials, both to be informed and in an effort not to second-guess the treatment plan

- Use positive words and think positive thoughts. Every day is a new experience and may bring all kinds of feelings to the surface

- Call family, friends and church for prayers of support and healing

- Schedule meals during treatments and/or surgery (See **Meal Calendar** in USEFUL TOOLS, page 92)

- Use **Medication Chart** (See USEFUL TOOLS, page 93)

- Use **Care Calendar** to organize additional support (See USEFUL TOOLS, page 89)

- Help with loved one's children: pick up/drop off for school, practices, parties; make lunches; do laundry, etc.

- Encourage positive mental imagery and physical relaxation techniques to avoid dark dreams

- Provide easy access to music/radio: set up CD, MP3, Stereo, or iPod, etc. Check out meditation, and inspirational and classical recordings

- Concentrate on positive life changes, (food, people, job)

- Make a gift of an electric blanket, which helps regulate body temperature

- Throw a "Soft Hat" Party at which everyone gives a special hat to their loved one

- Call loved one every other day to show positive support

- Give a small gift or card after each treatment for inspirational support

- Start or continue to seek spiritual support from a church community and/or services

- Watch funny movies together

- Subscribe to a new magazine or home-delivery DVD rentals

- Some people may lose their hair during treatment. Having the kids, a spouse, a friend or a hairdresser shave the hair before it all falls out might be an empowering experience for your loved one. Friends and family members may also choose to shave their head to show support

- Gifts of hats, scarves, and earrings are great ways to boost your loved one's morale

- Use **Fundraising Ideas** (See USEFUL TOOLS, page 90)
- Encourage and join in with simple exercises (check with doctor!)
- Plan a fun activity or trip to look forward to
- Hold hands
- Consider joining a support group
- Make an appointment for loved one to receive a massage
- Throw a Healing Party: invite your pastor and special people in your life to come together, so they can lay their hands on loved one's head and shoulders to say a prayer for their healing (Get permission from loved one first.)
- Use **Monthly Support Calendar** (See USEFUL TOOLS, page 98)
- Organize a fundraiser for loved one and family
- Celebrate the end of treatments with lunch or party
- **Avoid** these clichés! They really don't help someone going through truly tough times — in fact, for many people they create sense of failure.
  - This is nothing
  - You'll breeze right through it
  - Be tough
  - It's no big deal
  - I know what you are going through
- **Avoid** telling sad or negative stories to loved one & family members

Resources:
- American Cancer Society: *www.cancer.org*
- Children's Cancer Society: *www.childrenscancerassociation.org*
- National Breast Cancer Foundation: *www.nationalbreastcancer.org*
- Social Security: *www.ssa.gov*

DISEASE/ILLNESS

When we feel love and kindness toward others, it not only makes others

feel loved and cared for,

but it helps us also to develop inner happiness and peace.

— DALAI LAMA

AIDS/HIV

When my co-worker was diagnosed with AIDS I was shocked. I can't even imagine what was going through his mind, when he told the office staff. As time went by he seemed to become very fragile, with no energy, and withdrawn. One morning he came into the office and I asked him if he needed anything. His reply was "just a hug". I jumped up out of my chair and gave him a long, tight hug. After he left for the day, I rallied all the co-workers together and asked that, when our friend comes into work, we all give him a hug. They all smiled and said, "Great — he needs them." It was heartwarming. Staff members seemed to find the right time during the day to give him a quick hug. This went on for months, and you could tell he loved every hug he received. He wasn't alienated anymore and felt that everyone wanted to share their love and support for him.

DEDICATED TO OUR FRIEND

PARKINSON'S DISEASE

The most difficult outcome of my diagnosis has been the nearly total loss of my ability to play guitar. But, as it turns out, Parkinson's is also one of the best things that ever happened to me. Sure I'd rather play the guitar as I used to than tremble my way from chord to chord. But I believe that there is good in everything, and the good I've taken from this disease, so far, outweighs its negative effects. For one thing, I've learned to pursue my dreams. I've recorded a CD of my music with other people playing the guitar parts, and I've learned to bring character to my performances through my new, growly Parkinsonian voice. I've also learned to slow down, enjoy my moments, take naps, walk with gratitude, and laugh at myself. Parkinson's has made me humbler and, therefore, I hope, wiser and a better songwriter and teacher, a better husband and father.

— ROB BARTELETTI

POLIO

As a child I was diagnosed with polio. My father and mother knew my potential; in spite of my disease, I still could be all I wanted to be. I enjoyed skiing, hiking and, to this day, swimming. I have even been blessed with three beautiful children.

I appreciate it when people ask me why I have braces or crutches instead of whispering behind my back. I think to myself, my legs may not be perfect, but I can still use them.

I just wished people wouldn't treat me differently; everyone has an issue or disability, mine's just more obvious.

Thank you to all the people that see ME, my spirit, my personality, not my disease.

— BERNITTA SCHOENHEIT

Bedside Manners:

- Keep in mind, your loved one is not the disease
- Send flowers, cards filled with positive words, inspirational poems, prayers of healing
- Offer to drive and sit with loved one during treatments or appointments
- Offer to be the second set of ears at their doctor appointments, and bring a note pad with a list of questions, e.g. details of treatment plans
- Use medication pill box to organize different medication
- Use **Medication Chart** (See USEFUL TOOLS, page 93)
- Read the latest research, studies, papers, testimonials. Stay current on new developments in the understanding and treatment of your loved one's disease/illness
- Use **Care Calendar** (See USEFUL TOOLS, page 89)
- Help with your loved one's children: pick up and drop off for school, practices, parties; provide lunches, do laundry
- Schedule meals during treatments and or surgery. (See **Meal Calendar** in USEFUL TOOLS, page 92)
- Concentrate on positive life changes, (food, people, job)
- Organize a work party to build ramps and or install handrails etc.
- Provide easily accessible music/radio: set up CD, MP3, Stereo, iPod, etc. Check out meditation, and inspirational, and classical recordings
- Start or continue to seek spiritual support from a church community and/or services
- Be careful about the words you use. Every day is a new experience and may bring all kinds of feelings to the surface
- Throw a Healing Party: invite your pastor and the special people in your life to come together so they can lay their hands on your loved one's head and shoulders and say a prayer for their healing. Be sure to get permission from loved one first!

- Subscribe to a new magazine or home-delivery DVD rentals
- Join loved one in doctor-recommended exercises
- Talk loved one through visualizing movement of extremities
- Join local walks to support cures for the disease
- Make a gift of an electric blanket, which can ease body aches
- Hold hands with loved one; pray together, include children
- Join a support group, perhaps with your loved one. Find supportive computer chat rooms; visit loved one, by phone, and in person
- Watch funny movies together
- Use **Monthly Support Calendar** (See USEFUL TOOLS, page 98)
- Be a good listener; be patient with loved one
- Organize a fundraiser for loved one and family (See **Fundraising Ideas** in USEFUL TOOLS, page 90)
- Loved one may be inclined to choose a treatment that prolongs life in order to make family members feel better. Talk about this together — gently, but frankly and compassionately
- Loved one may depend on cane, walker, oxygen, etc. more for psychological than physical support. Accept that this is OK
- EXPECT A MIRACLE!
- Communicate with friends and neighbors for support
- **Avoid** telling sad or negative stories to your loved one
- **Avoid** these clichés! They really don't help someone going through tough times — in fact for many people they create a sense of failure
    - This is nothing
    - You'll breeze right through it
    - Be tough
    - It's no big deal
    - I know exactly what you are going through

29

Resources:
- ❖ Disease information: *www.righthealth.com*
- ❖ Mayo Clinic: *www.mayoclinic.com*
- ❖ Parkinson's information; *www.parkinsonsreasources.org*
- ❖ American Diabetes Association: *www.diabetes.org*
- ❖ National MS Society: *www.nationalMSsociety.org*
- ❖ American Heart Association: *www.americanheart.org*

DYING

I say to people who care for people who are dying,

if you really love that person and want to help them, be with them

when their end comes close. Sit with them — you don't even have to talk.

You don't have to do anything but really be there with them.

—ELISABETH KUBLER-ROSS

DYING

My Mother was from Ireland and a very dedicated Catholic. Mother, twin sister and I were asked to pray for our dying neighbor. Their nationality was Japanese and their religion was Buddhist.

My Mom lit a candle and set her cross and holy water on the bed-side table,all of us prayed together regardless of our different faiths and backgrounds.

The family felt the compassion and support from our prayers, and the Japanese neighbor lived for another three good years!

— MARGARET O.

~ ❦ ~

BEDSIDE MANNERS:

- Send flowers, cards, filled with positive words, inspirational poems, prayers of healing
- Visit as much as possible, and keep in contact with home-care personnel
- Don't let your own emotional upset make you careless or tactless
- Tell loved one how much you care for them
- Talk about good memories
- Hold hands and just be there
- You may want to invite a spiritual leader to visit your loved one and family
- Stroll around the block or garden and smell the flowers
- Don't miss this opportunity to tell loved one that they are loved
- Look at pictures together

- Read books to loved one
- Tell jokes, laugh together
- Make a meal for the family and a special dessert for loved one
- Gift a special candle for family and loved one to use near the bedside
- Take the time to express what makes your loved one so special, and to say your goodbyes
- Pray together
- Make a video or a recording of loved one's messages to the family
- Loved one may find it comforting to write letters to family members, especially concerning important future events
- Sew a quilt using personal shirts, ties, aprons, and jerseys, picture transfers, etc.
- Take pictures with kids, pets, family and friends
- You are out of town? Mail a card once a week with pictures and special notes inside
- Schedule a visit to fit in with care and /or family requirements. Children may be fearful to see dying person. Reassure them, it is normal to feel nervous
- If appropriate, assist in organizing finances
- A family member may want to discuss with loved one preparation of a living will or advanced directives
- Gently discuss the topic of being an organ/tissue donor, if no disease is present
- Talk with family about funeral services; loved one may want to plan service or have special requests
- If children are involved, family or head helper may want to notify teachers and coaches of situation
- Reassure loved one that everything will be taken care of: home, children, pets, self
- Play music that your loved one likes

Resources:

❖ National Mental Health of America: *www.mentalhealthamerica.net*

❖ Hospice Foundation of America: *www.hospicefoundation.org*

❖ Advanced Directives: *www.doyourproxy.org*

DEATH

Death is simply a shedding of the physical body,

like the butterfly coming out of a cocoon.

It is a transition into a higher state of consciousness,

where you continue to perceive, to understand, to laugh,

to be able to grow, and the only thing you lose is something

you don't need any more…your physical body.

It's like putting away your winter coat when spring comes.

—Elisabeth Kubler-Ross

Death

*During the challenging time of my Father's death, our family re-
ceived cards and meals from our friends. Every day we had a new
card to open or a nice fruit basket, even a giant chocolate cake!*

*It made the day a little brighter to know that we have such caring
friends.*

— David J.

~ ❦ ~

Bedside Manners

Before the funeral:

- Volunteer if needed to make phone calls. Make sure
  persons that you are calling are sitting down or, if driving,
  pulled off the road before you deliver the news that
  someone has passed away
- Send a card to express your condolences, for example:
  - We are so sorry to hear about your loss; your family is
    in our thoughts and prayers
  - I just heard the sad news about your friend's death, I
    send you much love & sympathy for your pain and loss.
  - Allow me to extend my heartfelt sympathy to you and
    your family
  - Remember, I am here to help any way I can; just call
    any time (your number here)
  - There are no words to take away the pain; just know
    that I am here for you day or night
- Send flowers to home or funeral parlor (ask florist for
  recommendations of types of flowers or plant.)
- Hugs are a great way of showing that you care

- Pray together, find a special prayer for the deceased
- Plan to attend memorial and /or funeral services, to pay your respects to the deceased and to support the surviving family and friends
- Prepare food for family: any meal, snacks, dessert, dinners, breakfast or lunch. Attach a card expressing your support
- Offer to help during the service: be a greeter, lector, minister; write and read a nice story about the deceased
- Start or continue to seek spiritual support from a church community, and or services
- Offer to construct or help with a display board of photographs of the deceased and family, starting from birth on
- Collect, then display at funeral home or reception, special poems, awards, medals, artwork, details of hobbies, that were favorites of the deceased and family
- Bring home movies for family members to view. Assess emotions for the right time to do this or leave with the family for them to view when they are ready
- Prepare food for reception. Church organizations my do this, or you may choose to have it catered
- Make hotel reservations if you are coming from out of town to attend services and give support
- Provide transportation for friends and/ or family that may be coming in from out of town
- If there is a viewing or rosary service, it is OK to request special arrangements before the service, for example:
  - Quiet time with the deceased
  - Special outfit for the deceased, e.g. glasses, hat
  - Religious statues and or medals
  - Candle to represent the light of God
  - Music (soft, special songs)
  - Flowers
  - A special blanket the deceased used
  - Display of a portrait of the deceased

DURING THE FUNERAL:

- Attend the funeral service
- Attire should be appropriate, as if you were attending church or a professional occasion
- Listen to family members, and be understanding
- Respect and observe the family's customs
- Allow yourself to just be present, under no pressure to participate in the ceremonies

AFTER THE FUNERAL:

- After services, offer to bring flowers to reception and or home. The family may want to leave flowers at church for services or donate plants to local residential-care facilities
- Be available to surviving family members: call, visit, bring lunch or a dessert
- Understand that tears and the full range of emotions are natural to the process of grieving and healing
- Be aware of the psychological stages of grief:
  - Denial/Shock
  - Pain/Anger
  - Sadness/Loneliness
  - Acceptance
- The healing process is different for every individual and can take a very long time
- Laugh and cry together
- Suggest or give materials on ways to cope
- Make frequent phone calls and visits over the next several months
- Allow surviving family members to share their memories of the deceased, and share your own that are positive
- It is all right to use the deceased person's name is conversations
- Encourage support groups if needed, and attend in support of loved one

- Use **Support Calendar** (See USEFUL TOOLS, page 98)
- Invite loved one to stay at your home for a few days, or longer
- Take children to the park
- Acknowledge birthdays, holidays and anniversaries
- Make a monetary contribution to the deceased person's favorite charity or start up a scholarship fund
- As weeks and months go by, the surviving family members need to know that you are still there for support
- **Avoid** statements such as these, which do not help at best, and cause pain and anger at worst
  - You'll get over it
  - The worst is yet to come
  - Others have survived it
  - Be strong
  - I know just how you feel
  - Did he or she leave you anything?
  - Time takes care of everything
  - You're young; you will meet someone else
  - At least his or her suffering is over
  - At least you have other children

Resources:
- Elisabeth Kubler-Ross Foundation: *www.ekrfoundation.org*
- The Veterans Health Administration: *www.va.gov*
- Social Security: *www.ssa.gov*

DEATH OF A CHILD

My daughter Jennifer was and still is an Angel. She was two and a half when she drowned in a backyard pool.

She had brown hair and blue eyes, full of energy; she was smart and loved everyone. I spent every waking minute of the day with her in the hospital. The doctors advised me of her grim future, that she might or might not come out of her coma and if she did, she would most likely require serious life-support. No way to ever really know. I relied on my faith to guild me in the decision to keep her on machines or let her go to heaven. A priest accompanied me in this most challenging time. I held her in my arms and said my goodbyes.

Much comfort came from knowing that some of Jennifer's organs would be used by other children that desperately needed them.

She loved balloons, so at the funeral service, we had bouquets of balloons all around the church. After the service the priest asked all the children to grab a balloon, and bring it to the burial site, to release them there. After everyone arrived at the cemetery, the children released the balloons simultaneously, as the priest said "Catch them, Jennifer, catch them" It was beautiful.

As days slowly went by, I felt as if I was dropping into a deep dark place. I went to church, hoping and praying that my God would help me. As I prayed with an aching heart, I felt my daughter's hands in mine, her voice telling me "Mommy it is time for you to smile" I then realized she was at PEACE.

As months and months went by, I continued to see a counselor who specialized in grieving. The counselor asked me "Why don't you ever cry?" I answered, "I need to stay strong" and the counselor replied with a statement that changed my life as I knew it. "Did you know what happened the day your daughter died? You died along with her." At that moment, I couldn't stop the tears; the tears covered my entire face. I felt free to live my life, to remember life is for the living. Jennifer and I without a doubt will see each other again.

— BERNITTA JONES

~ 🦐 ~

BEDSIDE MANNERS

HELP FOR THE FAMILY:

- Hugs are a great way to show you care
- Acknowledge the painful reality. Say, "I am here for you and your family "
- Plan to attend memorial and / or funeral services, to pay your respects to the deceased and to support the surviving family and friends
- Include loved one's friends in funeral ceremonies if they choose
- Notify school, daycare, after-school care and coaches of what has happened
- Ask the student body to hold a vigil for the loved one
- Ask teachers and / or student body to write a special note to the family / their classmate

- Send a card to express your condolences, for example:
  - We are so saddened to hear about your loss. Your family is in our thoughts and prayers
  - I just heard the sad news about your daughter/son I will cherish our memories together
  - Allow me to extend my heartfelt sympathy to you and your family
  - Remember, I am here to help in any way I can. Call anytime (your number here)
  - There are no words to take away the pain, just know that I am here for you day or night
  - I send you much love and sympathy for your pain and loss
- Offer to help during the funeral service: be a greeter, a lector, or write and read a nice story about the deceased child
- Start or continue to seek spiritual support from a church community and or services
- Offer to construct a display board of photographs of the child's life and the family, starting from birth
- Collect for display at the funeral home or reception, special poems, awards, medals, statues, etc., relevant to favorite hobbies, and interests of the child and the family

HELP AFTER THE FUNERAL:

- Be present for the family: call, bring lunch or a dessert by on a set date
- Understand that tears and a wide range of emotions are natural to grieving process, which involves several distinct phases: denial/shock; anger/pain; sadness/loneliness and, ultimately, acceptance
- Understand that the healing experience is unique to each individual and can take a very long time. Be patient
- Allow the parent/parents to decide when and if to clean out the child's room and what to do with personal items
- Screen telephone calls with an answering machine. The family may want to have quiet time
- Visit the burial site with friends and or family
- Prepare a gift basket with materials on ways to cope, such as books, inspirational plaques and a card
- Encourage the family to find outside mentors for siblings. A good place to look may be the Big Brother or Big Sister programs
- Encourage support groups if needed, and attend with family members for support
- Allow friends and family to share their memories and express their emotions; crying is a way of healing, so cry, cry, cry and laugh together
- Use the deceased child's name
- Remember birthdays and holidays. Together with neighbors light a battery operated colored candle for the deceased child and put it in the window on a favorite holiday or birthday
- Set off fireworks on the deceased child's birthday; put notices in the newspaper acknowledging special occasions
- Have a special Mass said at church for your loved one
- Assure the siblings/parents that they are not alone, they are LOVED

- Use **Support Calendar** (See USEFUL TOOLS, page 98)
- Demonstrate compassion for the family, not pity; watch your body language
- Assure siblings/friends that they have done nothing wrong
- Don't miss an opportunity to say "I love you" to everyone in your own family
- Don't let your own emotional upset make you careless or tactless
- **Avoid** statements such as these:
  - You should be over it by now
  - It's time you moved on
  - The worst is yet to come
  - Others have survived it
  - Be strong
  - I know just how you feel
  - How old was your child?
  - You should have taken better care of your health (in the case of a lost pregnancy)
  - You have other children

Resources

- National Sudden & Unexpected Infant/Child Death & Pregnancy Loss: *www.sidscenter.org*
- Parents of Murdered Children: *www.pomc.com*
- Elisabeth Kubler-Ross: *www.ekrfoundation.org*

DEATH OF A YOUNG PARENT

My father's death was a setback in my life. I was thirteen when my mother held me tight telling me what happened. I just kept telling myself that this was not possible. I felt numb all over. It wasn't real. My faith had been shaken. I kept on blaming God, believing that He did not have a purpose for taking my father from my family. My mother during this horrific tragedy showed much strength and courage. She stood up on both her feet and told me that things happen for a reason, and as hard as it may seem, it was my father's time.

I embraced my mother's attitude and grabbed onto my religion with all my strength. It helped me in so many ways, along with the support of my family and friends.

— JACOB, 16

BEDSIDE MANNERS:

HELP FOR THE CHILDREN AND FAMILY:

- Hugs are a great way to show you care
- Acknowledge the painful reality. Say "I am saddened to hear about your loss"
- Plan to attend memorial and /or funeral services, to pay your respects to the deceased and to support the surviving family and friends
- Attire should be appropriate, as if you were attending church or a professional occasion

- Allow children or teenagers to participate in memorial and funeral services if they wish
- Notify school, daycare, after-school care and coaches of the situation
- Arrange for the student body to hold a vigil for their bereaved classmate
- Ask teachers and/or student body to write a special note to the family/their classmate
- Send a card to express your condolences, e.g.:
  - We are so saddened to hear about your loss. Your family is in our thoughts and prayers
  - I just heard the sad news about your Mom/Dad. I will cherish our memories together
  - Allow me to extend my heartfelt sympathy to you and your family
  - Remember, I am here to help any way I can, just call any time (your number here)
  - There are no words to take away the pain, just know that I am here for you day or night
  - I send you much love and sympathy for your pain and loss
- Offer to help during services: be a greeter, a lector, or write and read a nice story about the deceased parent
- Start or continue to seek spiritual support from a church community and/or services
- Offer to construct a display board of photographs celebrating the life of the parent and his or her family
- Collect for display at funeral home or reception, special poems, awards, medals, statues, etc., relevant to favorite hobbies and interests of parent and family

HELP AFTER FUNERAL SERVICES:

- Be present for the family: call, bring lunch or dessert by on a set date
- Understand that tears and a wide range of emotions are natural to the grieving process. This involves several distinct phases: denial/shock; pain/anger; sadness/loneliness, and, ultimately, acceptance
- Understand that the healing experience is unique to each individual and can take a very long time, and be patient
- Visit the burial site with child or children of the deceased
- Suggest or give materials on ways to cope
- Encourage outside mentors, such as the Big Brother or Big Sister programs
- Allow friends and family to share their memories and express their emotions. Crying is a way of healing, so cry, cry; laugh and cry together
- Use the deceased parent's name
- Encourage support groups if needed, and attend with members of the family for support
- Remember birthdays and holidays.
- Together with neighbors light a battery operated colored candle for deceased parent and put it in the window on a favorite holiday or birthday; set off fireworks on the deceased parent's birthday; put notices in the newspaper acknowledging special occasions
- Have a special Mass said at church for your loved one
- Assure children and other family members that they are not alone, that they are LOVED, and that they have done nothing wrong
- Seek out an academic tutor if student needs to catch up on his or her studies
- Demonstrate compassion for the family, not pity; watch your body language

- Use Support Calendar (See USEFUL TOOLS, page 98)
- Don't miss an opportunity to say "I love you" to everyone in your own family
- Don't let your own emotional upset make you careless or tactless. **Avoid** statements such as these:
    - You should be over it by now
    - It's time you moved on
    - The worst is yet to come
    - Others have survived it
    - Be strong
    - I know just how you feel
    - How old was your Mom/Dad?
    - Time takes care of everything

Resources:

- Comfort Zone Camp: *www.comfortzonecamp.org*
- Elisabeth Kubler-Ross: *www.ekrfoundation.org*
- The Veterans Health Administration: *www.va.gov*

PET LOSS

Living with animals can be a wonderful experience, especially if we choose to learn the valuable lessons animals teach through their natural enthusiasm, grace, resourcefulness, affection and forgiveness.

— RICHARD H. PITCAIRN

MY CAT

It did not feel good to lose my cat Lucky. I named her Lucky because she was dumped at a golf course and so, I figured she was lucky to find me. I could bring her home to people that would love her and take good care of her. About 5 years later she was outside and got hit by a car and killed.

Now she is in a better place, maybe playing with my Grandpa in heaven.

My Papa and I made a cross for her burial site and we painted the name "Lucky" on the cross and we buried her at the golf course where I found her.

I know someday a long time from now, we will be together again.

— MICHAEL AGE 8

MY DOG

Annie was a sixteen–year-old Golden Retriever. She was named after Orphan Annie, due to the fact we adopted her from the Humane Society at 4 months old. Annie was the All-American Golden Retriever. Loving, devoted, obedient, and special to everyone she came in contact with. As she grew older, her quality of life remained good, until one day she collapsed on the lawn and with her sad eyes said that she was tired and ready to go. My parents offered to take her to the veterinarian and have her put to sleep. We didn't want Annie to suffer; we loved her way too much to let that happen. So as a family we decided to have my parents take her to the clinic, and on the way my mother fed her pieces of steak and treats. I guess in a way it was her last supper.

Our family is thankful for the support we received during this difficult time.

DEDICATED TO ANNIE

~ ❧ ~

BEDSIDE MANNERS

WHEN A PET IS DYING:

- Offer to bring the pet to the veterinarian to accompany it through the euthanizing process
- If possible, give other family members the opportunity to say good bye
- If appropriate, offer water, soft food to the pet. Call veterinarian for advice
- Brush fur gently; give lots of love, petting, holding

- Put a blanket over the pet
- Say "I love you" and thank the pet for its loyalty and companionship
- If appropriate, set a small fan on low to provide a cool breeze for the pet
- Sing a song to the pet, light a candle and pray over the pet

AFTER THE DEATH OF A PET:

- Send a card to the pet owner or the family in support
- Make or buy a cross/plaque/statue for home or burial site
- Give an opportunity for loved one to talk about the pet
- Tell them that you are sorry for their loss
- Present a picture of the animal in a special frame
- Some bereaved pet owners may choose to keep the ashes of the animal in a special box or vase, or to bury their pet in a special place, such as the family garden, or to spread the pet's ashes over a field or other favorite place of the animal. Be supportive of these choices, not critical!
- Do not minimize the pain of the bereaved pet owner
- Avoid such remarks as:
    - "The animal was in pain anyway"
    - "That animal was worthless"
    - "Just go get another one"

Resources:
- Pet Loss: Ten tips on coping *www.pet-loss.net*
- Pet Bereavement Counseling: *www.deltasociety.org*

Injury/Accident

What life means to us is determined not so much by

what life brings to us as by the attitude we bring to life;

not so much by what happens to us

as by our reaction to what happens.

— Lewis L. Dunnington

ATV ACCIDENT

It was a nice summer day when our family arrived at our ranch to ride the ATV's. Wearing our helmets of course, we would time our runs down and back on this dirt road. This one particular run, we noticed that my brother was way over his normal time. 15 minutes or so after he was due back, we all started to experience knots in our stomach. My family decided to drive down the dirt road and look for him. There he was, white as a ghost, barely walking. Being a very intelligent guy, he had kept his boot on and had been able to make a crutch out of a tree branch. Apparently, he had made a sharp turn, causing him to lose control; his ankle had collided with a stump sticking out of a large tree and he had been thrown several feet in the air, resulting in a crushed ankle and a broken collar bone. After his surgery he was laid up in bed for several weeks. His classmates came by every day with his school work, and some great conversation.

This act of kind friendship definitely helped him with his speedy recovery.

DEDICATED TO BILL

AUTO ACCIDENT/BRAIN INJURY

As my eyes opened, I read the sign on the wall: "Oregon Health & Science University". I reached up and felt a dozen steel staples in my head. I had been in a car accident that left me with a brain injury and several broken bones. I was not able to remember the accident or understand the significance of what happened. I lay in the hospital bed, full of different medications. I found it difficult to recognize people coming and going.

After a few days I began to recognize my sister and her comforting tone of voice. This helped me to begin to orient myself to my surroundings.

One of the keys to my recovery was my family and friends watching over and supporting me through my hospital stay and for many months after.

They asked questions of the hospital staff to better understand how to assist me. They requested that my pain medication be given to me in a timely manner. My sister encouraged me to cooperate with the nurses and treatments.

— TERESA O.

BEDSIDE MANNERS:

- The injured person may not recognize your face. Be patient
- Speak slowly and directly to loved one
- Bring only positive energy to your visits with loved one
- Pray in waiting room or chapel
- Request the hospital Chaplin to visit with you and your family
- Offer to be the second set of ears at appointments; bring note pad and pen and be prepared to ask questions on behalf of your loved one, for example:
  - How long will the procedure take?
  - Who will come out and tell me how he or she is doing?
  - When will I be able to see him or her after surgery?
  - What medications will be given and why?
  - What are the possible side effects?
  - What is the maximum amount that can be taken?
  - What foods are recommended, or to be avoided?
  - What options are available for in-home care?
- Consider donating blood for loved one
- Spend time with loved one before surgery (pray, laugh, hug, hold hands)
- Walk with your loved one to the surgery suite; let them know you are right outside the door
- Visit loved one in ICU or Recovery room. Be prepared for some difference in appearance, and leave young children with a babysitter
- Offer to take a shift at the hospital, so the family can get some sleep
- Treat loved one as if they are healing, not stupid
- Set up home with home-care equipment: hand bell, recliner chair, walker, cane, wheelchair, shower stool, special handle in restroom, ramp, clothing that is easy to get in and out of, with elastic and/or Velcro fastenings

- Remove area rugs
- Organize a work party to build ramps and or install handrails, etc.
- Arrange for childcare and pet care
- Use **Medication Chart** (See USEFUL TOOLS, page 93). Provide pill box and tablet cutter
- Prepare meals: breakfast, snacks, lunch, and dinner. Use **Meal Calendar** (See USEFUL TOOLS, page 92)
- Arrange for phone by bed/chair with answering machine on
- Call family, friends, church for prayers and support
- Offer to drive and sit with loved one at appointments and/or treatments
- Send flowers, and cards filled with positive words, inspirational poems, prayers of healing
- Provide easily accessible music/radio; set up CD, MP3, Stereo, iPod, etc. Check out meditation, inspirational, classical recordings
- Be patient: sleep is good for healing
- Be positive in words and actions; avoid negative or sad stories!
- Investigate alternative therapies, such as acupuncture, animal therapy, therapeutic touch, light therapy, massage, aromatherapy
- Seek out an academic tutor if student needs to catch up on his or her studies
- Post an oversized calendar with appointments and visitor information, e.g. **Care Calendar** (See USEFUL TOOLS, page 89)
- Investigate State assistances programs that may aid in the cost and or care of your loved one
- Consider hiring a retired nurse, nurses assistant or neighbor to help care for your loved one, while at work, appointments or when needing a break
- Post signs for Privacy and Rest.(See USEFUL TOOLS for **Privacy Cut-Outs**, pages 96–97)

- Gift Ideas:
  - Flowers, books, magazines, balloons, fruit basket
  - Nonskid socks, robe
  - New blanket for bed, cheerful pillow case
  - Poster with pictures of family, friends, animals etc.
  - Subscription to home-delivery DVD rental or a new magazine
- Help with shopping, house work, yard work etc.
- Keep in touch with loved one: call, visit
- **Avoid** these clichés! They really don't help someone going through truly tough times — in fact, for many people they create a sense of failure:
  - This is nothing
  - You'll breeze right through it
  - Be tough
  - It's no big deal
  - I know what you are going through

Resources

- Mayo Clinic: *www.mayoclinic.com*
- American Red Cross: *www.redcross.org*
- Brain Injury Association: *www.biausa.org*
- The Veterans Health Administration: *www.va.gov*
- Amputee Coalition of America: *www.amputee-coalition.org*
- National Spinal Cord Injury Association: *www.spinalcord.org*

Mental Health

When you reach out to hurting people, that's when God is going to make sure your needs are supplied. When you focus on being a blessing, God makes sure that you are always blessed in abundance.

-Joel Osteen

ALZHEIMER'S DISEASE

Alzheimer's is a strange journey for the patient and the people who love the patient.

In the case of my 85-year old mother, my siblings and I shared the experience openly and lovingly, and relied on each other along the way. It was not easy, but any load that is shared is lighter. Our mother was living alone when we started to notice changes.

Her calls became more frequent and redundant.

Balancing her checkbook had become difficult; simple math was now a challenge to her.

We started with a gerontology exam at the hospital. My older brother, sister and I sat with her as the doctor laid out the grim prognosis. Mom seemed indignant and defensive about the assessment. She didn't want to be a burden to anyone. My siblings and I worked together to make decisions that we believed were in mom's best interest. We found a Memory Care Center devoted to Alzheimer's patients. It was pleasant, with activities and music every day. She lived there for three years, losing more of herself each day until she was 90. At the end, she was a near empty vessel of herself. We gathered over her as she drew her last breaths. Her three remaining children, holding hands and praying together. It was a powerful moment.

I'm so glad I had my mom as long as I did.

MONICA CORY

BEDSIDE MANNERS:

- When behavioral changes occur with loved one, seek medical advice
- Be the second set of ears at appointments; bring note pad, pen and a list of questions
- Educate yourself, family and friends on the nature and progress of the condition
- Investigate State assistances programs that may aid in the cost and or care of your loved one
- Consider hiring a retired nurse, nurses assistant or neighbor to help care for your loved one, while at work, appointments or when needing a break
- Speak slowly and directly to loved one
- Loved one may not recognize your face. Be patient
- Bring only positive energy to your visits with loved one
- Remembering may be difficult for your loved one; try to bear with mental changes
- Out of town family and friends may call once or twice a week
- Set up home with home-care equipment: hand bell; recliner chair; walker; cane; wheelchair; shower stool; easy-use door-handle in restroom; ramp; easy on/off clothing with elastic and/or Velcro fastenings
- Remove area rugs that are likely to slip
- Set up an oversized calendar to chart appointments and visits
- Use **Medication Chart** (See USEFUL TOOLS, page 93), pill box and tablet cutter
- Help with shopping, house work, yard work, etc.
- Prepare meals: breakfast, snacks, lunch, dinner (See **Meal Calendar** in USEFUL TOOLS, page 92)
- Place phone by bed/chair with answering machine on
- Hang pictures of family where loved one can view them easily

- Call family, friends, church for prayers and support
- Send flowers, cards filled with positive words, inspirational poems, prayers of spiritual healing
- Provide easily accessible music/radio: set up CD, MP3, Stereo, iPod, etc. Check out meditation, inspirational, and classical recordings
- Read to loved one each week
- Family or friends may want to set up a schedule for outings once a week (See **Care Calendar** in USEFUL TOOLS section, page 89)
- Investigate alternative therapies, such as acupuncture, animal therapy, therapeutic touch, light therapy, massage, aromatherapy
- Assist with balancing check book or finances
- Power of Attorney may be needed
- Locking file cabinet for important papers and personal items may be needed
- **Privacy and Rest signs** can be used (See USEFUL TOOLS section, pages 96–97)
- Keep in touch with loved one: call, or visit, often
- Visit and compare Memory Care facilities to find the best match for your loved one. Enquire about:
  - Cost
  - State Board of Health check
  - Staff Background checks
  - Security; monitored living
  - Visitation policy
  - Well-being checks on loved one
  - Medical staff at facility
  - Injury policy; notification
  - Meals
  - Activities
  - Transportation
  - Chapel

- Keep in touch with your religion
- Treat loved one with respect and dignity

Resources:
- Mayo Clinic: *www.mayoclinic.com*
- Alzheimer's Association: 24 hour help line #1-800-272-3900 *www.alz.org*
- National Mental Health of America: *www.mentalhealthamerica.net*
- Advanced Directives: *www.doyourproxy.org*

DEPRESSION

The best support I received was from my Mom. When I tried to commit suicide as a teenager, she reminded me of how much it would devastate her if I succeeded; that the people I left behind would be the ones to suffer forever due to my selfishness. It was tough to listen to. Then about six years ago my medication stopped working and they changed my meds to a "higher class". Within 24 hours of taking my new meds, I was suicidal. My husband took me to the hospital and expressed to my mother that he was tired of the ups and downs and was thinking of leaving me. When the doctor heard this he pulled my husband aside and asked him, "If your wife had cancer, would you leave her?" The doctor was very firm with him, told him this was no different, this was a disease that I did not want to have.

I have found that phoning my "help lines", these being the people that love me, works best. If I didn't have my family and friends, my life would be dark. I rely on them for my lift: it's supportive to be around people that understand and want to help. People need to reach out to those they know are suffering from depression and let them know they care and they are not alone! That what they have is a DISEASE, not a choice.

— DEANNA A.

POST-TRAUMATIC STRESS DISORDER, OR PTSD

The hardships were many and unexpected: five months after I entered the service I was in Vietnam. The training was minimal and there was no training to cope with the harshness and violence of the war. Most soldiers created emotional barriers to protect their emotions and to forget the painful sights of each day. Soldiers needed to escape from the reality of the war: some used alcohol, some used drugs, some isolated themselves and withdrew from the world.

When I returned to the US, I was transported from the plane to a processing center for release to go home. Four hours after I landed, I was in my father's car headed home. There was no debriefing or preparation for what we would encounter from society in general. A large portion of the public scorned the Vietnam veteran. The emotional barrier was activated again and most people thought the veteran was emotionally unbalanced, when this was his defense mechanism for survival. When the vet would or could not talk about the war and the stories of nightmares circulated, this created doubt about their stability. The government, pressured by the public, started an investigation into the actions of the soldiers in the war. This made many veterans, afraid to talk about the war, keep their emotions inside. Many vets could not handle this and went off the deep end, abusing alcohol and drugs, and committing suicide.

Today we have a similar situation in Iraq and Afghanistan. I have been told that our soldiers are better prepared physically and mentally to cope with the war. Remember, when these soldiers come home, give them respect and love, and help them to adjust to society. Let the soldier talk about the war and listen, as they need to speak at their own pace without the feeling of pressure, and understand these people have been through an emotional turmoil. Seek out material on Post-Traumatic Stress Disorder and other issues that may arise.

This is your country and these individuals have chosen to be the ones to protect us and execute the policies of our elected officials.

DEDICATED TO 7/17 AIR CAV.

~ ❧ ~

BEDSIDE MANNERS:

- Encourage medical attention; drive loved one to clinic or hospital
- Educate yourself with relevant information about the condition: the internet can be a great source
- Self-inflicted harm may be a serious cry for help. Seek medical attention immediately

- Encourage counseling to improve the mental health of the individual and/or the whole family
- If the depressed person refuses to get help, you should acquire useful tools to help loved one, by attending counseling yourself. Use the **Monthly Support Calendar** (See USEFUL TOOLS section, page 98)
- For someone who is lonely, consider a pet. Educate yourself on the needs of any new pet
- Consider setting up a routine to pray together
- Volunteer at a local soup kitchen or homeless shelter together
- Help with basic household chores
- Volunteer to paint a room in their house a new color
- Join a Health Club together
- Stay in touch with loved one, call, visit, plan a day trip, and reach out
- Let your loved one know that you care, remembering that actions speak louder than words
- Help with positive life changes
- Avoid negative statements and actions, especially those belittling the pain, or minimizing the situation, such as:
  - Your experience is in the past
  - It's all in your head
  - It's time you got over this

Resources:
- National Mental Health of America: *www.mentalhealthamerica.net*
- National Suicide Prevention Lifeline 1-800-273-8255: *www.suicidepreventionlifeline.org*
- U.S. Department of Veterans Affairs: *www.va.gov*

Special Assistance

Love knows no limit to its endurance, no end to its trust,

no fading of its hope; it can outlast anything.

Love still stands when all else has fallen.

—Author unknown

ASSISTED LIVING

Nana was up in her years and needed assistance with daily living. So, she moved in with our family of six. She was an independent woman who wanted to do things on her own. She would forget to take her daily medication, snap at the kids, and complain about most everything. After a year, we decided as a family, including our beloved Nana that she needed to be moved into a senior assisted-living facility. It was hard to come to that chapter in our lives. However, we knew it was best for the health and wellbeing of our entire family.

— DEDICATED TO NANA

~ ❦ ~

BEDSIDE MANNERS:

- Investigate State assistances programs that may aid in the cost and/or care of your loved one
- Consider hiring a retired nurse, nurses assistant or neighbor to help care for your loved one, while at work, appointments or when needing a break
- Gently tell your loved one about your plan, focusing on the positive reasons for it
- Some families may choose to have relatives take turns in having loved one move in with them.
- If moving to a care-facility is the only option; clearly explain the positive reasons for the move: these may include improved safety, better healthcare, more compatible company, even the restoration of a measure of independence. Be compassionate in responding to your loved one's concerns. Practice patience, and pray on it

- Consult with your loved one in choosing an assisted-living facility: work together to satisfy your loved one's preferences and budget. Is there a choice of facilities near family, church, stores? What insurance coverage, state funding or savings are available?
- Before you visit, make sure that the parent companies of the facilities on your list have a good history in assisted/senior housing and are licensed
- When you visit, ask about the following:
  - State Board of Health check
  - Staff Background checks
  - Security/Safety
  - Visitation policy
  - Well-being checks on loved one
  - Medical staff at facility
  - Injury policy, and notification
  - Meals
  - Activities
  - Transportation
  - Chapel
- Get confirmation of the information you receive
- Respect your loved one's attachment to personal belongings
- Work together as a loving family during this change
- Power of Attorney may be needed; see website support at the end of the chapter
- Use locking file cabinet for important papers and personal items
- Use **Monthly Support Calendar** (See USEFUL TOOLS section, page 98)
- Mail a card once a week
- Create a routine to visit your loved one. This is very important to the whole family (include children)

⚲ Does your loved one need to prepare a Living Will and/or a Medical Directive Form? (See website support at the end of the chapter)

⚲ All family members need to pitch in with moving, visiting, and staying overnight if needed

Resources:

❖ National Mental Health of America: *www.mentalhealthamerica.net*

❖ Public legal forms: *www.publiclegalforms.com*

❖ Advance Directives: *www.doyourproxy.org*

CHILD WITH SPECIAL NEEDS

From the very first moment we saw Alivia, we were aware she was born with Downsyndrome. No one could actually speak it aloud, instead acting happy and excited that our grandchild was finally born. We took pictures and smiled, tears lingering, ready to explode. My daughter finally looked at me and said, "It's true isn't it?" I said, "Yes, it's true". We cried. We knew Alivia was a very special gift, but at that time we were completely unaware of how much of a fit she would be for us. With only a few complications, far fewer than for many babies with Down syndrome, our daughter and son-in-law were able to finally take her home. The hospital had given us several lists of things to watch for and possible complications that might arise. We were all afraid. We bought books and read everything we could about Down syndrome.

We also read real stories of how people coped.

Not only did many people know "nothing" about Down syndrome, they also used the word "retarded", which truly startled us. At no time did that ever come into our thoughts.

Within a year, we could see that Alivia was able to grasp so much that we taught her.

As grandparents, we are thankful for this beautiful granddaughter who helps us stretch and become better people. To think....we were so afraid.

— LORRAINE ROBBINS (GRANDMA)

~ ❧ ~

BEDSIDE MANNERS:

- Consider seeking a second opinion if not satisfied with diagnosis
- Write down questions, to bring to doctor/therapist appointments. Educate yourself and others on the specific disability. Use the internet, take classes, etc.
- Allow everyone time to emotionally process the diagnosis
- Share the news of the disability with family and friends and form a circle of support
- Find a support group, through the hospital, the internet, local organizations
- Use medication pill box to organize different medications
- Ask medical staff or therapist about home-care equipment
- Educate yourself about, your state's Early Intervention programs
- Learn Sign Language
- Investigate State assistance programs that may aid in the cost and or care of your loved one

- Consider hiring a retired nurse, nurses assistant or neighbor to help care for your loved one, while at work, appointments or when needing a break
- Attend parent/children get-togethers organized by associations for various disabilities
- Prepare meals for the family (See **Meal Calendar**, in USEFUL TOOLS section, page 92)
- Use **Monthly Support Calendar** (See USEFUL TOOLS section, page 98)
- Use **Care Calendar** to help support the family (See USEFUL TOOLS section, page 89)
- Use **Fundraising Ideas** (See USEFUL TOOLS. page 90)
- Help with basic household chores
- Avoid meaningless, negative or unanswerable statements and questions!
  - But they are so loving (all children are loving)
  - How slow will he/she be? (every child is different)
  - How mentally challenged will he/she be? (pray for a miracle)

Resources:

- Northwest Down Syndrome Association: *www.nwdsa.org*
- Autism Research Institute: *www.autism.com*
- Mayo Clinic: *www.mayoclinic.com*
- Parenting Special Needs Children: *www.specialchildren.about.com*
- Special Olympics: *www.specialolympics.org*

SURGERY

Only through experience of trial and suffering

can the soul be strengthened, vision cleared, ambition inspired,

and success achieved.

— HELEN KELLER

WHEN A CHILD HAS SURGERY

I was born without a nerve in my right cheek. When I was four, surgeons took a nerve from my right leg and transplanted it to my cheek. When I was six, surgeons took a muscle from my leg and put it in my cheek and hooked it up to the nerve. Without that transplant, one side of my face would droop down and would never have been able to be fixed. The thing that kept me going was the support from my family. They gave me cards, stuffed animals, that sort of thing. It was hard to be stuck in one room with very little to do.

— DANIELLE R. AGE 10

~ ❧ ~

BEDSIDE MANNERS:

- Ask the doctor/medical staff about the procedure, medications, side effects, therapy
- Consider donating blood for loved one
- A parent or other may want to stay the night with the child, if resources allow. Offer to stay, allowing the parent to get some sleep and re-charge
- Let child know that everyone is praying for him/her
- Provide a set of ear plugs to improve loved one's night's sleep
- Provide music: set up CD, MP3, stereo, iPod, etc., with a choice of meditation, inspiration and classical
- Take charge of meal preparation for the family during treatments and or surgery (See **Meal Calendar**, USEFUL TOOLS section, page 92)
- Visit loved one in hospital room (be prepared for a possible difference in appearance)

- Visitors should limit their time with loved one while in the hospital recovery process (leave small children at home with a babysitter)
- Offer to drive to appointments or hospital so parent can assist child
- Use medication pill box to help with organization of different medications
- Call family, friends and church for prayers and support
- Use positive actions and words to promote healing
- Privacy and Rest signs can be used to help with recovery period (See **Privacy Cut-Outs**, USEFUL TOOLS, pages 96–97)
- Transport siblings to school or activities
- Seek out an academic tutor if student needs to catch up on his or her studies
- Call the family home and wish loved one a speedy recovery (see **What Do I Say**, page 8)
- Possible Gift Ideas:
  - Visits to the loved one
  - A card or letter from friends, family and/or classmates
  - Small stuffed animal
  - Bouquet of flowers or balloons
  - New colorful pillow case
  - Comfortable non-skid socks, or PJ's
  - Collage of pictures, of friends, family and pets
  - Story, picture or joke book
  - Age-appropriate movie
  - Coloring packet
  - Power bars for parents or next of kin
  - A "Feel-Good Bag" with special gifts inside for child to look at during treatments and or recovery

Resources:
- ❖ Mayo Clinic: *www.mayoclinic.com*
- ❖ St. Jude's Hospital: *www.stjude.org*

DAY SURGERY

During my husband's surgery, I was sitting in the family waiting room at the hospital, hoping the surgery and recovery would be without any complications.

My cell phone rang, it was a friend, and she said "I will take your children home after school, feed them dinner and bring them home in time for bed."

It was such a relief to know that they were taken care of and I could be with my husband in the recovery room.

MONICA J.

BEDSIDE MANNERS:

- Send flowers, cards, filled with positive words, inspirational poems, prayers of healing
- Offer to drive and sit with loved at clinic or hospital
- Offer to be the second set of ears for their doctor visits. Bring note pad with questions, about procedure and what to expect
- Use medication pill box to help with organization of different medications
- Read about the latest research, studies, papers, testimonials on recovery
- Prepare a meal or two (See **Meal Calendar** in USEFUL TOOLS section, page 92)
- Start or continue to seek spiritual support from a church community and or services
- Call family and friends for prayers of healing
- If patient needs in-home assistance, offer to stay and help, possibly over a period of time
- Set up any in-home aid for loved one i.e. shower stool , cane
- Drive patient to follow-up appointments
- Turn music on at home
- Music, set up CD, MP3, Stereo, iPod, etc. (meditation, inspirational, classical)
- Set up answering machine, send an e-mail on loved one's status
- Concentrate on positive life changes, (food, people, job)
- Subscribe to a new magazine or home-delivery DVD rentals
- Keep in touch with loved one, call, visit

Resources:
- Mayo Clinic: *www.mayoclinic.com*

GENERAL SURGERY

We understand the power of prayer, and together we created a ministry to share the healing and support of prayer. It began when our father was recovering from a quadruple by-pass. We prayed for his quick recovery and called our friend, Sister Grace, to ask her to pray for our father's health. We prayed together on the phone, and Sister Grace's warmth, concern and affirmation through prayer contributed greatly to the comfort of our family and, we believe, to our father's astounding recovery.

So, moved by the experience, we started a prayer chain at church, feeling that all should have a "Sister Grace" to call upon when they need extra support.

The first call we received was for a man recovering from quadruple by-pass, the same situation as our father. We knew that request was a confirmation from God that prayer really works.

DEDICATED TO WILLIAM J. OLLENBROOK.

~ ❦ ~

BEDSIDE MANNERS:

- Offer to be the second set of ears at appointments; bring note pad and pen, and be prepared to ask questions on behalf of your loved one
    - How long will the procedure take?
    - Who will come out and tell me how he is doing?
    - When will I be able to see him after surgery?

- What medications will be given, and why?
  What are the possible side effects?
  What is the maximum amount that can be taken?
- What foods are recommended, or to be avoided?

⊙ Consider donating blood for loved one

⊙ Spend time with loved one before surgery (pray, laugh, hug, hold hands)

⊙ Walk with your loved one to the surgery suite; let him know you are right outside the door

⊙ Visit loved one in ICU or Recovery room. (Be prepared for a possible difference in appearance.)

⊙ Visitors should limit their time with loved one while in the hospital recovery process (leave small children at home with a babysitter)

⊙ Offer to take a shift at the hospital, so the family can get some sleep

⊙ Provide ear plugs to allow loved one a better night's sleep

⊙ Ask about the need for home-care equipment, e.g. hand bell, recliner chair, walker, cane, wheelchair, shower stool, special handle in restroom, ramp, clothing that is easy get in and out of, with elastic and/or Velcro fastenings

⊙ Use **Medication Chart** (See USEFUL TOOLS, page 93) Provide pill box and tablet cutter

⊙ Prepare meals: breakfast, snacks, lunch, dinner (See **Meal Calendar** in USEFUL TOOLS, page 92)

⊙ Arrange for phone by bed/chair with answering machine on

⊙ Call family, friends, church for prayers and support

⊙ Offer to drive and sit with loved one at appointments and or treatments

⊙ Send flowers, and cards filled with positive words, inspirational poems, prayers of healing

⊙ Provide easily accessible music/radio; set up CD, MP3, Stereo, iPod, etc. Check out meditation, inspirational, classical recordings

⊙ Be patient

- Be positive in words and actions; avoid negative or sad stories!
- Investigate alternative therapies, such as acupuncture, animal therapy, therapeutic touch, light therapy, massage, and aromatherapy
- Post a calendar in kitchen, with appointments and visitor information (See **Care Calendar**, USEFUL TOOLS, page 89).
- Post signs for Privacy and Rest (See **Privacy Cut-Outs** in USEFUL TOOLS section, pages 96–97)
- Gift Ideas:
  - Flowers, books, magazines, balloons, fruit basket
  - Nonskid socks, robe
  - New blanket for bed, cheerful pillow case
  - Poster with pictures of family, friends, animals, etc.
  - Subscription to home-delivery DVD rental or a new magazine
- Help with house work, yard work, etc.
- Keep in touch with loved one, call, visit
- Avoid these clichés! They really don't help someone going through truly tough times — in fact, for many people they create a sense of failure:
  - This is nothing
  - You'll breeze right through it
  - Be tough
  - It's no big deal
  - I know what you are going through

Resources:
- Mayo Clinic: *www.mayoclinic.com*
- American Heart Association: *www.americanheart.org*
- American Red Cross: *www.redcross.org*
- Amputee Coalition of America: *www.amputee-coalition.org*

VICTIMS OF CRIME

... In spite of everything, I still believe that people are really good at heart. I simply can't build up my hopes on a foundation consisting of confusion, misery, and death. I see the world gradually being turned into a wilderness, I hear the ever approaching thunder, which will destroy us too, I can feel the sufferings of millions and yet, if I look up into the heavens, I think that it will all come right, that this cruelty too will end, and that peace and tranquility will return again.

— ANNE FRANK

DOMESTIC VIOLENCE

As a young woman, dreaming of all I would accomplish after graduating from college, being an abuse victim was not anywhere on the list. Abuse victims were weak and not confident in who they were. That had nothing to do with me.

That was, of course, before I found myself years later, at the end of sixteen-year marriage to a man who had spent the better part of that time controlling, manipulating, and emotionally and mentally abusing me and our children. Our marriage was filled with tumultuous years of walking on eggshells to avoid violent outbursts.

This marriage finally ended unfortunately with a nightmare night of terrorizing threats and physical assault in which my 15-year-old son had to call 911 to save his and my life.

Immediately after this tragedy, with my soon-to-be-ex-husband in jail, I felt weak, broken and unable to focus on the future. My younger children were having trouble sleeping in our home, so we decided to move and start over where it wouldn't be easy for him to get to us if he was released.

As we settled into our new home, and mail was forwarded to me, I'll never forget the feeling opening some of the first letters from close friends. They were all addressed to "MY STRONG and BEAUTIFUL" friend.

Who are they talking to? How can they call me strong after what I just let happen all of these years?.

Reading these letters and talking to my dearest friends who know me the best reminded me often that I was strong and that was how I had endured for so long and had kept my children so healthy through all those tumultuous years.

— TRACI (STRONG & BEAUTIFUL)

HOMICIDE

She was 19 and beautiful inside and out, a young lady with many qualities and a whole life to look forward to. She had typical struggles that young people do when they are growing up. However, she had a unique struggle in her life. She was controlled and manipulated by a pimp, a young man who was evil. Her father and I tried to distance Diana from his life. It didn't work; he had her controlled and fearful. Several months later, I received the phone call stating that Diana had been found dead in California. I was in shock, numb and lifeless. Living in Oregon, I called the D.A.'s office and the Portland Police Department to learn what my next step would be. During this nightmare, I found the most support from the Portland Police and VICE Departments.

When I was at the lowest point, a special detective became the person I could lean on. He educated me on how pimps manipulate and control young girls with fear. I then met with a Captain of Portland Homicide. He would call me and say, "Let's walk at lunch so you can talk about your feelings, I know you must be under a lot of stress." I felt that they were my lifeline! My other saving grace was and still is the Portland Oregon Chapter of Parents of Murdered Children. I was fearful to walk through that door for the first meeting, because they were going to judge Diana and me. I walked through the door and found open and loving arms.

I have been walking through that door now for 22 plus years, supporting others in similar situations.

—GAYLE MOFFITT

~ ❦ ~

BEDSIDE MANNERS

HELP TO OFFER IMMEDIATELY:

- Educate yourself and loved one on the early signs of domestic violence
- Maintain a good balance of support for your loved one, keep communication lines open, healthy boundaries and don't turn away from your loved one. Ask loved one to trust your words and actions to help move them out of the troubled relationship
- Get the victim to a safe place, e.g. police station, hospital, family home
- Encourage victim to confide in a trusted friend or family member
- Call the police; wrap the victim in a warm blanket, and get medical attention
- Urge the victim not to remove, change, clean clothes, or shower until after police and medical investigation and examination
- As soon as possible, write down all the facts surrounding incident or assault
- Be sensitive and patient regarding the victim's feelings and emotions; be a good listener

- Missing person: make flyers of missing person and post in windows, stores, libraries, cars, etc.; join the organized search team and be available to work with the authorities

Help to offer the victim of a violent crime in the days following the incident:

- Treat your loved one as a loved one, rather than as a victim
- Offer practical assistance to help protect and empower your loved one
- Arrange a place to stay with family or a close friend
- Encouragement to get counseling, whether by phone, group or personal sessions
- Your company to the courthouse to request an Order of Protection
- Help with packing, moving and setting up house elsewhere, if that is an option
- Your offer to call employer to request time off work
- Help notifying neighbors and co-workers of the crime. Educate yourself and others about this type of crime
- Don't dwell on the situation or the past, but allow your loved one to tell their story, and listen
- Instead of offering advice, offer a vote of confidence: tell your loved one how wonderful he/she is, in order to counteract past negative comments
- If children are exposed to violence, help to find resources to assist in managing their sense of vulnerability. These may include writing in a journal, painting, praying, and talking with a counselor

Resources and Phone Numbers:

❖ National Domestic Violence Hot line:
   1-800-799-SAFE (7233) *www.ndvh.org*

❖ RAINN : Rape, Abuse and Incest National Network
   Hot line: 1-800-656-4673 *www.rainn.org*

❖ National Center for Victims of Crime:
   1-800-394-2255 *www.ncvc.org*

❖ Mothers Against Drunk Driving: *www.madd.org*

❖ National Center for Missing & Exploited Children:
   www.missingkids.com

USEFUL TOOLS

Sample Monthly Care Calendar for Loved One

You may want to fill in every day and give a copy to loved one and everyone who is supporting the loved one. Any calendar may be used for this. Just fill in the days as needed; each week may be different.

September 20___

SUN	MON	TUE	WED	THU	FRI	SAT
					1	**2** AM: Teresa PM: Next door neighbor
3	**4** AM: Aunt Lucy PM: Karen	**5**	**6** AM: Nancy PM: John	**7**	**8** AM: Maddy Noon: Monica PM: Nick	**9**
10 AM: Kristin PM: William	**11**	**12** AM: Katherine Noon: Papa PM: Jack	**13**	**14** AM: Aunt Dim	**15** Noon: Uncle Jim	**16** PM: Kaitlyn
17 AM: Danny	**18** Noon: Jessie	**19** PM: Bryan	**20** AM: Uncle Ed	**21** Noon: Next door neighbor	**22**	**23** Noon: Minister
24	**25** Noon: Lucy	**26**	**27** Noon: Maggie	**28**	**29**	**30**

89

Fundraising Ideas
to Provide Financial Support for Friends or Family in Crisis.

Art:
Sell paintings, clay creations, pottery, at a local weekend market, and/or your local college campus. Make sure to receive permission to do so.

Auctions:
e.g. a silent Auction and Picnic.

Bake Sales:
Outside of school or church, selling cakes, cookies, breads.

Bank Account:
Open a bank account for loved one and family, and let people know how they can make a deposit.

Candy Sale:
Purchase candy bars at your local grocery store and sell them at 100% mark up. Make a label, and attach it to the wrapper identifying your cause.

Car Wash:
Arrange to use gas stations, school, store parking lots.
To ask for donations is often more effective than charging a flat fee.

Coin Collection:
Collect coins from students, co-workers, parishioners, neighbors.

Direct Appeal:
E-mail people you know with an update on the situation, along with details enabling them to send money and/or gift cards.

Games:
Organize a Bingo Night, at which players buy cards, and prizes are donated.

Meals:
Hold a Chili Cook Off, a Spaghetti Dinner, Coffee & Doughnuts.

Plant Sale:
Ask a local nursery to donate plants, then sell them at discounted prices.

Pop Can Collection:
Ask people to bring their contributions to one location, or offer to pick them up and bring to a recycling center/pop can return.

Private Enterprise:
Help and supervise the neighborhood children to run a lemonade stand or play their instruments at your local Saturday market, with a donation box identifying your cause.

Raffles:
Car, travel vouchers, gift certificates, quilts, etc. Check with your state officials for guidelines.

Rummage Sales:
Located at church, school, and or backyards.

Sponsored Events:
Organize a walk with pledges per mile or lap; advertise the event in your local news media.

Sports Events:
Organize golf, bowling, tennis, soccer, softball tournaments, charging a participation fee and admission fees.

Proceeds go directly to the person and/or family in need.

Sample Meal Calendar for Loved One

Any calendar may be used for this — just fill in the days as needed. Meal needs may vary according to family size and situation. Meals may be delivered to loved one's home. If this is a family of your child's classmate, drop off meal at school so eldest child can take it home after school. Pass calendar around or drop off at school to be filled out; make copies for school, for you, and for loved one.

September 20___

SUN	MON	TUE	WED	THU	FRI	SAT
		You may want phone numbers in addition to names, for reminder calls.	Questions: Call (name) ___ ___ - ___		1	2 Dinner: Aunt Rose Meatloaf
3	4	5 Dinner: Wilson family	6	7 Dinner: Uncle Bill Baked Chicken	8	9 Dinner: Church ladies
10	11	12 Dinner: Smith family	13	14 Dinner: Adams neighbors	15	16 Dinner: Sister Grace
17	18	19 Dinner: Mollahans Irish Stewf	20	21 Dinner: Reynolds family	22	23 Dinner: Wilson family Spaghetti
24	25	26 Dinner: Ollenbrooks	27	28 Dinner: Whites Pizza	29	30

Medication Chart

Keep all medications out of reach of children and pets.

Name _____ Age _____ Blood Type _____ Date _____

Condition _____ Physician _____ Insurance # _____

Allergies _____ Emergency Phone _____

MEDICATION NAME/STRENGTH (Generic/Therapeutic Equivalent?)	PURPOSE / Directions	Amount/ Frequency	Times of Day					WARNINGS / Notes Side effects? Activities to avoid? Food requirements?
			AM	Noon	PM	Bed	As needed	

Natural Remedies

Consult your healthcare professional for advice before using natural remedies which may conflict with prescribed medication, and carefully read labels for directions on how to use them properly.

All these remedies may be found at health food and grocery stores.

Bleeding, Shock, First Aid

- Capsicum tablets: bleeding, shock, nose bleeds
- Bach's Rescue Remedy: shock, anxiety
- Arnica gel: reduce bruising after fall or injury
- Baking soda: poison ivy, sunburn.
  Mix with bath water or make paste

Broken Bones:

- Liquid Calcium, added to shake or fruit smoothie in the evenings

Constipation:

- Aloe Vera juice: liquid or capsules
- 6 – 9 glasses of water per day
- Glycerin suppositories
- Eat fruits and vegetables

Diarrhea:

- Bentonite Clay, hydrated or powdered:
  follow directions on the bottle until elimination is normal
- 6 – 9 glasses of water per day
- Activated Charcoal: for food poisoning
- Acidophilus tablets: to replenish good bacteria in the gut

Insomnia:

- Chamomile tea
- Melatonin capsules
- Exercise
- Lavender Lotion

Nausea:

- Raspberry tea
- Papaya juice or tables
- Peppermint essential oil: 1 drop on the tongue or diffused in air

Pain:

- Arnica: gel, tablets or homeopathic
- Cold and hot packs
- White Willow Bark
- Epsom Salt bath: for adults add ¾ cup of Epsom Salt to bath water. Drink 2 – 3 glasses of water during bath
- Cool damp wash cloth on forehead

Respiratory Congestion:

- Colloidal Silver: for colds and flu
- Eucalyptus essential oil: 2 – 3 drops in warm bath or diffused in air
- Fenugreek and Thyme, in tablet form: help relieve congestion
- Saline solution: flush sinuses

Skin Irritations:

- Golden Salve
- Baking Soda mixed with bath water or make paste
- Aloe Vera gel

Supportive Treatments:

Ask your healthcare professional for advice if you are interested in trying these treatments.

- Acupuncture
- Therapeutic touch
- Massage
- Animal therapy
- Magnetic therapy
- Light therapy
- Hydrotherapy

Privacy Cut-out #1

We are resting today.

We want to thank you
for stopping by and showing
your support.

Please write your name on
the list below.

Have a great day.

_____

_____

_____

_____

_____

Please,
Do Not Disturb
at this time.

Thank you
for your
consideration.

Sample Monthly Support Calendar for Loved One

You may want to fill in every day and give a copy to loved one and everyone who is supporting the loved one. Use any calendar for this. Confirm loved one's address.

September 20___

SUN	MON	TUE	WED	THU	FRI	SAT
					1 Mary mails an inspiration card	2
3 Neighbor drives friend to church	4 Grace drops off breakfast	5	6 Bill calls and talks with loved one	7 Drive to the store and window shop together	8 Paint a picture together	9 Ben makes dinner
10	11 Watch Monday Night Football together	12 Dave stops by with herbs to plant in the garden	13	14 Maddy delivers dessert	15	16
17 Nick picks up loved one for church	18 Mike mails a card	19	20 Jon mows the lawn	21 Drive to the beach	22 Monica mails a card	23 Make an apple pie together
24	25 Put a puzzle together	26 Teresa calls with good news	27 Take a walk together	28 Keith stops by with lunch	29 Mail a card with a funny joke written in it	30

Name_____   Address_____

Medical Information Cards

PRIMARY CARE PHYSICIAN

Name _____

Hospital/Clinic _____

Phone _____

Fax _____

Address _____

Email _____

PHARMACY

Pharmacy _____

Phone _____

Fax _____

Address _____

Email _____

Account Number _____

SPECIALIST

Name/Specialty _____

Hospital/Clinic _____

Phone _____

Fax _____

Address _____

Email _____

SPECIALIST

Name/Specialty _____

Hospital/Clinic _____

Phone _____

Fax _____

Address _____

Email _____

HEALTH INSURANCE

Company Name _____

Agent's Name _____

Phone _____

Fax _____

Address _____

ID# _____

SECONDARY HEALTH INSURNACE

Company Name _____

Agent's Name _____

Phone _____

Fax _____

Address _____

ID# _____

ADVANCE DIRECTIVE/ORGAN DONOR

Person who has the Advance Directive _____

_____

Phone _____

Oregon Donor Information _____

_____

EMERGENCY CONTACTS

Name _____

Phone _____

Name _____

Phone _____

Name _____

Phone _____